THE MODERN
RULES OF
Business
ETIQUETTE

THE MODERN RULES SERIES

THE MODERN RULES OF

Business

ETIQUETTE

DONNA GERSON AND DAVID GERSON

AMERICAN BAR ASSOCIATION
Defending Liberty
Pursuing Justice

Cover design by ABA Publishing.

13 12 11 10   5 4 3 2

Library of Congress Cataloging-in-Publication Data

Gerson, Donna L. and Gerson, David A.
    The modern rules of business etiquette.
    Donna L. Gerson and David A. Gerson
Library of Congress Cataloging-in-Publication Data is on file.

ISBN: 978-1-59031-922-2

Eunice Burns (played by Madelyn Kahn):
"Don't you know the meaning of the word 'propriety'?"

Judy Maxwell (played by Barbra Streisand):
"Propriety ... Noun: Conformity to established standards of behavior, or manner, suitability, ripeness or justice. See etiquette."

From *What's Up Doc?* (1972)

Table of Contents

Preface

Could a book about etiquette for lawyers be a bit like a book about vegetarianism for a tribe of cannibals? We think not and disagree (politely) with anyone who assumes otherwise. While there are certainly a number of excellent books on manners for the general public, there are no recent resources that discuss etiquette and the legal profession specifically.

Our *Modern Rules of Business Etiquette* will teach you the not-so-secret secrets of how to behave like a proper gentleman or lady who is also an officer of the court. Why should the rules of etiquette concern lawyers? Good manners are, simply put, good for business. No matter how brilliant your legal brain may be, if you fail to treat others with respect and kindness, then you will not enjoy the professional success you desire. Don't believe the hype: Nice lawyers—and talented professionals—finish first.

In *Modern Rules of Business Etiquette* you will learn the rules of good manners and the pitfalls of bad behavior, from the time you interview, to partnership, and beyond. Our twelve easy-to-read chapters provide practical guidance and tips for everyone, from the entry-level associate to the most senior partner. After all, it's never too late to be polite.

What qualifies us to write this book? A reasonable question, no doubt. David is a partner in the business and finance practice at a major international law firm, and spends his days (and many nights) in continual telephone, email, and face-to-face contact with clients, other lawyers, staff members, outside consultants, transaction counterparties, and opposing counsel. He sees the theory and practice of formal and informal systems of etiquette and conduct—and their positive and negative impacts—every day. Donna is a contributing editor for *Student Lawyer* magazine and writes extensively about legal career issues. She lectures at law schools across the U.S. When visiting law schools, Donna meets law students and learns first-hand about the issues, controversies, and concerns on the minds of students, hiring partners, and career services professionals. Both Donna and David have witnessed first-hand some truly appalling manners in their many travels.

We've been married nearly twenty years and have been exceedingly polite to one another with some notable exceptions that don't bear repeating here (no matter how funny they are in hindsight). While good manners are not the sole key to our success, we believe they do count as a big plus in our lives. (Just ask our son, whose lot in life is to be reminded of the rules of etiquette constantly by us both, to his evident joy.)

We do hope you enjoy this book and gain a better understanding of the importance of good manners. We welcome your comments so long as they are considerate in tone and well-written. Donna is a sparkling presenter and witty raconteur, and would be pleased to speak at your law firm, bar association, or law school. (David's billable hourly rate is . . . oh, never mind.) Thank you for your consideration and happy reading.

Donna and David Gerson
Pittsburgh, Pa.

Interview Etiquette

Your job interview sets the tone for future employment. While your academic credentials and work experience are factors taken into consideration by an employer, your behavior throughout the interview process will spell success or failure as a job candidate.

Stories abound regarding interview actions that smack of poor behavior, thoughtlessness, and lack of common sense. A candidate with stellar credentials who is nonetheless a boor will bear the consequences of his poor behavior. Conversely, the competent academic candidate with excellent interpersonal skills and evidence of a strong work ethic may be able to sway a hiring partner's decisionmaking process in his favor.

The following tips will help you navigate the interview process and capitalize on your credentials.

Résumé

Your résumé provides an employer with relevant information about your academic successes, work experience, and other achievements of interest. Typically one page in length—one page for every ten years' work experience—

your résumé should be printed on plain white or beige paper. Avoid brightly colored paper, wild graphics, or anything that will draw attention to your résumé in a negative way.

Be sure that your résumé is free from misspellings, typographical errors, and any puffing. Your goal is to present your information as accurately and plainly as possible. Keep font choice simple and consistent. Times New Roman font is easy to read, as are Garamond and Arial. Font size should be at least 11-point, ideally 12-point; anything smaller will be difficult to read. In addition, as more employers move to scanning technology to digitally read résumés, a consistent font and font size will simplify your application process.

If you are emailing a résumé to an employer, consider sending the document not only as an attachment but also in the body of your message. Despite the formatting irregularities that may result, you guarantee that a potential employer will be able to review your credentials quickly rather than waste time trying to open an attachment. A simple note saying, "For your convenience I have attached a copy of my résumé for your review and have also pasted it into the body of this message in case you have difficulty opening the attachment. Please forgive any formatting irregularities as the result of emailing this document to you."

Cover Letter

Your cover letter ought to be three or four paragraphs that succinctly introduce you to an employer and describe your relevant credentials without reciting your résumé in its entirety. A well-written, personalized cover letter should convey your reason for seeking employment and highlight particular skills or experiences that may be of interest to an employer. As with your résumé, avoid typographical errors, grammatical errors, or misspellings.

Writing Sample

Many employers request writing samples, particularly from law students and recent graduates. A writing sample offers an employer a sense of your writing style and enables you to have a discussion on a specific legal topic. Generally speaking, writing samples ought to be between five and ten pages in length. If you have a longer writing sample (for instance, a longer brief with three separate issues under consideration), then consider choosing one issue for presentation to an employer. A short paragraph at the beginning of the writing sample can explain that this represents one of several issues before the court.

Of course, your writing sample must be wholly your own work and not the result of a collaborative project or excessive editing by a faculty member. In addition, know the content of your writing sample backward and forward. If you cannot discuss intelligently the issues presented in your own work, then you cannot expect an employer to have confidence in your ability to do the job.

References

Many employers ask for two or three references either before or during the interview process. Choose individuals who know your work product and your work ethic. Always ask a reference for permission to be listed as a reference *before* you interview. This way, no one is taken aback or surprised by a phone call or email requesting information about you.

Your Internet Presence

In the age of MySpace, Facebook, and personal blogs, employers have been known to Google candidates and find information unintended for a larger audience; to wit, photos from your bachelorette party, a blog that you wrote during law school, or candid observations posted online by your ex.

Your email address should reflect a professional demeanor. Hence, no email addresses such as *sxylwyr@gmail.com* or *barelylegal@yahoo.com*. Keep it simple, business-like and neutral: your first initial and last name or first and last name.

If you maintain a personal web page, make sure that it exudes professionalism and good taste. Nothing can be hidden on the Web, and employers—as well as clients—will question your good manners (and good judgment) if they find tasteless, thoughtless, or inflammatory information posted by you or about you.

Before you embark on the interview process, Google yourself to see what comes up. If you find unwanted material about yourself, then you may need to engage the services of a company such as ReputationDefender (*www.reputationdefender.com*) to de-optimize certain entries and create other entries for employers to find.

Scheduling the Interview

When an employer or staff member calls to schedule an interview, you are "on stage" going forward. Accordingly, your manners—good, bad or nonexistent—will be scrutinized from now on. The moment the email arrives or the telephone rings to arrange a time to meet, you must exercise proper etiquette. Proper etiquette means:

A Prompt Response

When you are interviewing, consider yourself "in play" 24/7. This means regular checks of your voice mail (home and mobile phones), email, and regular mail. Long lapses responding to employers will be considered a sign of indifference and translates into bad manners. The day you receive an invitation to interview, respond immediately.

An Enthusiastic Response

When you respond, do so with enthusiasm. Nothing creates a bad impression faster than the candidate who calls with an attitude to schedule an interview. While you should not act fake, you should summon a level of enthusiasm about the prospect of receiving an interview and convey that to a potential employer. "Thank you for the letter inviting me to interview with your firm. I would be delighted to schedule a time to visit your offices," goes a lot farther than "Oh, I guess I have to schedule a time to come in now."

Plan Ahead

When scheduling an interview, be sure to ask for directions (if it's not a location with which you are familiar) and reiterate to the person with whom you are speaking about the date, day, and time. Some employers—judges, for instance—might ask job candidates to research and draft a short brief as part of the interview process. Plan ahead and ask. Also, ask if the employer needs any additional information at the time of the interview: for instance, a writing sample, transcript, list of references, or other documentation. Remember: proper planning prevents poor preparation.

Reimbursement for Travel

If an employer offers to reimburse you for travel to an initial or second interview, review the parameters for reimbursement. What is covered? Does the law firm handle the travel and hotel arrangements or does the interviewee? To whom should receipts be sent? Is there a form that must be used? What is the timeline for reimbursement? What are reasonable costs for the purposes of reimbursement? Understanding these details helps avoid any misunderstandings that can be construed as poor etiquette. Countless stories are told of interviewees who displayed poor etiquette—and did not receive a job offer as a result—due to reimbursement requests for nightclub visits, adult movies on Pay-Per-View, or raiding the mini-bar at the hotel.

Conduct Research

Before arriving for your interview, research the employer to understand its key practice areas, significant cases, representative clients, and recent news about the firm. This information can be obtained through a simple Internet search, or by using Westlaw or LEXIS/NEXIS®. By understanding key information about your potential employer, you can formulate intelligent questions, convey information that may be relevant to a potential employer, and form a positive first impression.

If you are given the names of the lawyers with whom you will be interviewing, also take the time to research basic information: college, law school, practice areas, key cases or deals, any publications, or noteworthy awards. While the roster of lawyers you will be meeting with may change on short notice, at the very least you can be familiar with many of the people with whom you will be meeting and can plan ahead.

Arrive on Time

If you have planned ahead, then you should arrive on time (translation: about ten minutes before the interview start time but no earlier than that). Tardiness will be viewed negatively and conveys both poor etiquette and poor planning on your part.

Appropriate Dress

In most cases, interview apparel will consist of the traditional dark-colored suit, white shirt, conservative shoes, and minimal jewelry. Tattoos and body piercings (other than earrings for women) should be covered discreetly from public view.

When faced with the dilemma of business casual, opt for a more formal rather than a less formal attire. Too casual can be misconstrued as not serious. Carry a briefcase or portfolio containing extra résumés, writing samples, transcripts, and a list of references.

A Firm Handshake

The appropriate mode of greeting during an interview (or any business situation for that matter) is a firm handshake. It may sound silly, but practice shaking hands to make sure your handshake is firm, but not bone-crushing, and that your hand is dry, not clammy. You may not wave hello to people in interviews, nod your head in their general direction, or bow at the waist. Extend your right hand with confidence and shake the other person's hand in greeting while saying, "It's a pleasure to meet you."

Staff Relations

Treat everyone you meet during the course of your interview with the utmost respect and kindness. From the managing partner to the filing room clerk, every single person deserves to be treated with respect. The sign of a true lady or gentleman lies in the ability to treat every single person with the same level of deference, regardless of rank. Everyone deserves direct eye contact, a smile, and a handshake. Everyone you meet during the interview process will someday have to interact with you during a routine business day. Therefore, your interview day should be your opportunity to lay the groundwork for a mutually respectful work environment.

Ask Appropriate Questions

During the course of your interview, you will be asked by an employer, "Do you have any questions for me?" Unless you do not want to receive an offer, come prepared with questions to ask. "No, I don't have any questions," is not a proper response.

If you have engaged in research prior to your interview, then you ought to have several thoughtful questions to ask. Avoid asking questions that would involve a simple yes or no answer; instead, focus on asking questions pertaining to a person's motivation or reasoning. The following questions invite an employer to speak about substantive issues:

> *"What made you decide to practice labor law?"*
>
> *"Do you find that your mentor program helps retain promising lawyers?"*
>
> *"Tell me what you enjoy most about your work at this firm."*

Inappropriate questions are those that may embarrass, surprise, or call into question your work ethic. The essence of good etiquette is to put people at ease. Hence, avoid questions relating to marital status, race, religion, salary, vacation time, or parental leave. Issues relating to remuneration, billable hours, and benefits will be discussed in detail after the offer is made. In many cases, particularly with large firms, this information is publicly available from the *National Association for Law Placement (NALP) Directory of Legal Employers*.

Meals

During the interview process, candidates are typically taken out to lunch or dinner by members of the firm. The meal can be a chance to demonstrate one's excellent etiquette skills or showcase one's lack of good manners. To avoid the latter, here are some tips to guide you:

- Drink in moderation. One serving of alcohol at dinner will suffice. More than one drink and you may lose your focus. These days, imbibing alcohol at lunch is *verboten*. Follow the lead of the most senior person regarding alcohol consumption, but always err on the side of the teetotaler.

- Choose foods that are easy to eat. Avoid saucy or oily dishes, spaghetti, or anything that will splatter or drip.

- Engage in conversation. Your role in the interview meal is not to indulge in a fine meal (save that for another time), but to engage in delightful, relaxed conversation with potential colleagues. Stay alert and in interview mode throughout the meal.

- Do not order the most expensive dish on the menu. The interview meal is not the time to order the caviar or the chef's tasting menu (unless you're following the lead of your hosts).

- Despite the lovely atmosphere and the tasty meal, you are still interviewing—remain focused and do not lapse into too-familiar territory. Often firms will send associates who are close to you in age. You may feel relaxed and open to discussing things more openly than if you were with a more senior lawyer. Avoid becoming too familiar with your meal partners; this is still an interview.

- Use your table manners, always. Napkin on lap when you are seated. Water glass to your right. Bread plate to your left. Fork in your right hand. Knife in the right hand. If you need a refresher course in dining etiquette or feel nervous, get tutored beforehand.

Cocktails

Occasionally, when time is limited you will be treated to a drink at a local bar. Proceed with caution. One drink, if you consume alcohol, is probably the most you should enjoy while interviewing. After one alcoholic beverage, switch to club soda with a lemon or lime wedge. Loose lips may sink ships, but too much alcohol will derail your interview forever.

Say Thank You

"Thank you." Perhaps the two most important two words in the English language. Express your thanks both verbally and in writing. When you are leaving the restaurant or the office at the conclusion of your interview, shake hands with the interviewers and say, "Thank you, I'm so pleased we met and learned more about your firm." Within twenty-four hours, send a typed thank-you letter to the person who organized your interview (at large firms this person would be the legal personnel director). Depending on the circumstances, a handwritten note may also be acceptable. Email communications can be acceptable, too, depending on the age of the person with whom you are corresponding. Use your good judgment when drafting written or email communications, but in any event, convey your sincere thanks promptly.

Accepting an Offer

After successfully navigating the interview process, the next potential pitfall comes at the time you accept an offer. When you receive an offer, typically the hiring partner or human resources director will explain the terms of employment: your start date, your salary, benefits, and the like. The employer will also give you a deadline to accept the offer. While there is room to negotiate particular issues (although in the case of a recent law school graduate this is unlikely to be the case), you should honor the acceptance deadline. Ignoring the deadline or simply ignoring the offer are both signs of poor manners.

When faced with multiple offers of employment, follow the Principles and Standards for Law Placement and Recruitment Activities set forth by the National Association for Law Placement (*www.nalp.org*) regarding the number of offers that can be held at one time. When rejecting an offer, do so with care and sincerity. The law firm you reject today may be the employer of your dreams in two years.

When you do accept an offer, do so in a timely manner, in writing, and with enthusiasm. Nothing starts an employment relationship off on the wrong foot faster than mishandling the acceptance process.

Declining an Offer

When you must decline an offer, do so by telephone if at all possible, followed by an appropriate, typed letter. An email note declining an offer has the feel of informality, and is frowned upon by most recruiting professionals. Moreover, no matter how accurate your email program's spell-check function may seem to be, the chances of an error in an email are simply too great; while we all hope to have many choices of potential work environments, and, thus, the chance to choose not to work at one or more of them, there is no need to burn a bridge through a careless email containing typographical or grammatical errors that causes the rejected employer to say, "Good thing we didn't wind up taking that one; we dodged a bullet."

Rescinding an Acceptance

Avoid the drama of "cold feet" after accepting an offer of employment. This type of poor behavior will set a negative tone whether your ultimately accept the offer or rescind your acceptance. Whether you are seeking a job immediately following graduation or are switching firms mid-career, you ought to have considered all of the pros and cons before accepting an offer of employment. Retracting an acceptance reflects poorly on you as an individual and will not be forgotten.

Office Etiquette:
Working with Those More Senior

Law is a service business, within which our highest priority is to serve our clients. That priority extends from the most senior lawyer in each attorney-client relationship through the people in the mail room, and embraces everyone in between. Every successful lawyer recognizes that, while technical brilliance can carry you far down the field, service excellence enables you to cross the goal line.

The junior lawyer, especially when working in a larger, institutional setting, may be tempted at first to see clients as remote, other-worldly beings. In fact, though, clients are all around them; clients are behind the memos they write, the depositions they attend, the due diligence documents they review; clients are the recipients of the timesheet entries they compose; ultimately, clients are writing the paychecks they cash (and then promptly use to pay their law school debt). More immediately, junior lawyers have a separate, often insistent set of clients readily at hand: As a junior lawyer, the more senior lawyers with whom you work are your clients.

As with external clients, your primary goal in working

with those more senior than you should be to make the job of the more senior attorney easier, by being eager, appropriate, honest, timely, available, and responsive; the etiquette of working with more senior lawyers revolves around each of those specific behaviors. If you can master not just the substance, but also the style, of serving in a more junior role, then you'll truly squeeze the most out of each experience, quickly assume the higher levels of responsibility you seek, and at the same time gain valuable insights into how to manage client relationships and entire matters, and how to supervise more junior attorneys yourself someday.

Let's look at some specific situations in which junior lawyers often find themselves, and try to discern some of the "do's and don'ts" of working in a more junior role.

• "The Importance of Being Earnest"

Imagine that you're a junior attorney, recently embarked upon your career, sitting at your desk and waiting for the phone to ring (perhaps dreading that it will). When the call does come, don't answer with trepidation or resignation; put a smile on your face and a song in your heart, and say, "I'm happy to help in any way; I'll be right down." Come prepared; bring a pad and a pen at all times. Sit up in your chair. Look the assigning attorney in the eye. Pay rapt attention, look eager, and take good notes as the assignment is given.

Wait until the assignment has been laid out, then ask any questions that have occurred to you during the assignment meeting; there really are "no stupid questions," and you'll show respect for the external client by seeking to be efficient in resolving the obvious issues upfront. Before leaving, be sure to ask when the assignment is due, and when before then the assigning attorney wants you to check back with a preliminary report. Finally, tell the assigning attorney, "I'm sure I'll have additional questions as I get underway; what's the best time and way to reach you for clarification or guidance?"

In all of the foregoing behaviors—each of which is its own, self-contained little rule of etiquette—you'll convey the earnestness that says to a more senior attorney, "This person is on the ball; I'm in good hands."

• "Do you have a second?"

So, now it's a day or two later, and you're in the heart of the assignment, when suddenly you hit a brick wall; you need guidance in order to go on. Trotting down to the assigning attorney's office, you find a scene of loosely organized madness; a secretary is putting one caller on hold while the second line rings, there's a fresh six-inch stack of papers in the "in" box; hand-marked documents are strewn across the assigner's desk in various stages of completion; and the assigning attorney is hunched over a keyboard, clearly enrapt in tapping out an email.

In other words, you arrive *in medias res*; you're about to interrupt. In so doing, you're about to take the assigning attorney out of what he or she was doing—out of a particular frame of mind, thought process, and state of knowledge— and ask him or her to shift gears in order to re-enter your project, get up to speed on where you started and where you are now, understand the obstacle you're facing, and help guide you forward; in short, to switch gears completely, and at high speed.

Consider, instead, asking the secretary how you can secure a moment of the assigning attorney's time to help resolve an issue in your project. That gives the assigner the chance to resolve his or her crises in an orderly fashion, and devote more complete and thoughtful attention to yours.

You'll likely get a clearer, more helpful response, while at the same time not adding to the pressures on the more senior attorney. (Of course, if you're truly in meltdown mode, or up against a critical deadline, then interruption may be appropriate.)

The rule of etiquette here is not to presume that your own issue takes precedence, but to defer where possible to the more senior attorneys to prioritize the challenges they face—including the challenges you face on their behalf—in the way that most efficiently and effectively serves their external clients.

• "Mr. Corleone insists . . ."

What happens when the conclusion you reach appears to be different from the one that the assigning attorney expected? That happens; after all, if all of the answers were known or preordained, there would be no real reason to occupy you with finding them anew. Still, it can be disturbing, even terrifying, to feel as though you're about to deliver a different answer than was anticipated. What if you've uncovered something that causes a whole case or deal to move into uncharted territory? Worse yet, what if you're wrong? It's enough to make you want to sit in your office with the door closed, either staring at the phone or updating your resume, and many a junior attorney does just that.

In the classic film, *The Godfather,* the Don's *consigliere,* attorney Tom Hagen, tells someone who has failed to accede to the Don's wishes, "Mr. Corleone is a man who insists on hearing bad news immediately." Similarly, your rule of etiquette when you have bad news to deliver should be to do so immediately, and preferably in person. This is an instance where interruption is appropriate; moreover, it's one in which your ability to look the assigner in the eye and lay out your case can be critical in conveying the importance of what you have to say, and in helping the assigning attorney to access both your verbal and nonverbal cues in order to integrate the news and decide how to proceed.

At the very least, convey your conclusion by phone, if a face-to-face meeting isn't possible for some reason. Try to stay away from voice mail messages of bad news, and avoid email except as a last resort; as a communication medium, email lacks the ability to convey tone and nuance, and is thus uncommonly prone to misunderstanding at a time when concision and content are key.

• Better late than never . . . NOT

A handy guideline for both assigning attorneys, and those who work for them, is that everything takes longer than you think it will. When an assigning attorney says, "This should take you an hour or two," plan for more like four or six; if you finish early, then more's the better. (Note, though, that this is different from an assigning attorney saying, "Spend an hour on this and then report back." In that case, an hour means an hour, either because there's a looming deadline or a budget consideration—or both—and you should adhere to the restriction.)

Still, sometimes work really does expand beyond the time available for its completion, and, despite your best efforts, you're about to run late or, worse yet, you actually blow clean past the deadline. Many junior attorneys are tempted to conclude that, "If they aren't screaming for it, they must not need it," and to keep working—or just hide— until the project is finally done, or escape is impossible.

The rule of etiquette in this situation, however, is precisely the opposite: As soon as you perceive that a deadline won't be met, inform the supervising attorney immediately, and work out a new timeline. Hiding under your desk with a blanket, a flashlight, and a three-day supply of crackers will not avail you in these circumstances. While you're busy assuming that the assigning attorney really didn't need this when he said he did, he's busy assuming that you have it all taken care of, and what falls through the gap between those two assumptions is the interest of the external client, who may be prejudiced (or simply annoyed) by not receiving an answer when she wanted it.

• "Is anybody out there?"

Let's shift our scene somewhat, and enter the office of the more senior attorney. Amidst the tumult of her day, a thought comes into her mind, of her more junior colleague, toiling away on a project assigned to him earlier, and the thought is one that requires outreach—perhaps a status check, possibly a new fact that might be of help to the more junior attorney, maybe a change in the timetable for completion. The senior attorney sends a message, by email or voice mail, and receives back . . . nothing. No acknowledgment of receipt, no reply, just the sound of one hand clapping, and that hand is not attached to the arm of the more junior colleague.

What do you do when a more senior attorney (or anyone, for that matter, from the partner in charge to the peanut vendor) reaches out for you? The rule of etiquette is, "respond." A simple "got it" will serve, in many circumstances. When an attorney leading a project communicates with you as a team member, he's creating in his head a mental checklist item; by acknowledging the communication, and, if possible, reporting status, you allow the supervisor to tick off that item and move on to the next, thereby keeping the entire project on track. Silence here is not golden, it's merely unhelpful.

• "Where's Waldo?"

Staying with our theme of the more senior attorney searching out the more junior colleague, hardly anything can be more frustrating to a project leader than being unable to locate a team member when needed. This doesn't mean that you need to chain yourself to your desk, or take your BlackBerry to bed with you, but it does mean that you need to be capable of being located when you're likely to be needed. The rule of etiquette, then, is to let someone know how to reach you when you're away from your desk during normal business hours, or, outside business hours, when you would be expected to be reachable.

If you're going to lunch, tell your secretary, and give a sense of when you expect to be back; if you'll be in a meeting, let your assistant know whether you can be disturbed, and, if so, then for whom you *must* be disturbed; if you will be in the bathroom, washing your feet in the sink (a true story, but one for another chapter, or perhaps another book altogether), then either return quickly or leave a trail of bread crumbs so that you can be found in a pinch. In all events, accept that you're a part of a collaborative effort—and a key part, no matter how junior you may think you are—and accord your teammates the courtesy of being able to be located when required.

Office Etiquette:
Working with Peers

Work colleagues who are your peers are especially important to your career development. You will be traveling the same path with these people, moving forward in your careers. Some lawyers will view their peers as their competition. Resist the temptation to view your professional life through the lens of scarcity—if she advances in her career, I recede in importance.

Instead, focus on developing collegial relationships with your peers with the knowledge that the future is uncertain. Assume the attitude that you are part of a collective enterprise and everyone's success inures to the benefit of the firm. Moreover, lawyers move between firms with regularity, go into business for themselves, find positions in-house, or leave the professional entirely. Your work colleague today may be your client tomorrow.

Since you cannot know what the future holds, treat all of your peers with the respect and collegiality they deserve. By demonstrating simple kindness and respect for your colleagues, you elevate yourself and—at the same time—will create a reputation for kindness and decency that will extend beyond your time at a particular firm.

Avoid the Gossip Mill

There's a difference between gossip and intelligence-gathering. While it's important to understand the intricacies of office politics and to have a nuanced knowledge of who's good to work for and who ought to be avoided if possible, draw a bright line at idle gossip and avoid it whenever possible. One can say it's simply good manners not to talk about people behind their backs; you would not want people doing the same, so why engage in that type of behavior? You do not want to have a reputation among your peers as someone who is untrustworthy or indiscreet.

On the other hand, gathering information about law firm news—who may be a good mentor (or an indifferent mentor), and so forth—is an acceptable and, some would say, important skill to acquire. Know the difference between information-gathering and gossip and be scrupulous about not engaging in hurtful chatter, whether in person or online.

Share Information

Create a mutually supportive environment among your peer group by passing on information. For example, if you are aware of an upcoming continuing legal education class on a subject of interest or the opportunity to speak at a professional seminar, share that information with your peers. Creating a flow of information to others will help ensure that similar information will flow in your direction.

Create a Network

As you advance in your career, create a network of colleagues and become a referral source for information and ideas. Rather than hoarding names of potential client contacts, work together to build business and share expertise. You may specialize in labor and employment law, but you need a trustworthy peer who specializes in tax law in order to attract clients. The process of building silos between your firm's practice areas and peers will not benefit you or your firm in the long run. Be the person who creates the connections within your firm and beyond. Not only will your connectivity create value for your firm, but it will also benefit your clients.

Email and Blog with Care

When drafting or forwarding emails or using the Internet at the office, be sure to exercise caution before you hit "send." Many a relationship and reputation has been tarnished, sometimes beyond repair, from thoughtless emails, equally tactless forwarding of emails, and reckless blogging. Avoid flaming colleagues, belittling others in correspondence, or otherwise behaving in a fashion that would cause you grief later. Google "law firm sushi" and you get the picture.

Once you have committed words to email or the Internet, assume that they will forwarded and seen by everyone in the world. An excellent resource for lawyers to consult regarding email etiquette is *Send: The Essential Guide to Email for Office and Home* by David Shipley and Will Schwalbe.

Recognize Life-Cycle Events

When your peers get married, have children, or experience a loss, acknowledge these life-cycle events in a timely manner. This can be as simple as an email (although this may be a bit impersonal in some instances) or, ideally, a personal, hand-written note or greeting card.

Sending a greeting card to a colleague's home is a thoughtful way to show support for another person. Keep a variety of greeting cards or personal stationery in your office, along with stamps, so it's easy to jot a note and send it when you hear news. *Just a Note to Say ... The Perfect Words for Every Occasion* by Florence Isaacs (Clarkson Potter, 1995) offers excellent advice to help you draft meaningful notes. What you write does not have to be profound or perfect; simply put some sincere thoughts to paper and send it.

Some major life-cycle events worthy of recognition are:

Weddings

When you are invited to a colleague's wedding, respond to the invitation in a timely manner. Buy an appropriate present; if the couple is registered at a store, consider buying a gift from the wedding registry. Otherwise, money is always an appropriate wedding gift. Check with people for the appropriate amount.

Births or Adoptions

When a co-worker or colleague announces the birth or adoption of a child, take a moment and acknowledge this life cycle with a card or small gift. A few words of welcome are always appreciated. When considering a small gift, you need not spend a great deal of money. Many stores carry small items, or you can order a personalized piggybank or burp clothes online. While gift-giving is not required, it can be a kind gesture.

Deaths

When someone in your office experiences a death in his or her immediate family, good manners dictate that you acknowledge your colleague's loss. Send a sympathy card as soon as possible with a personal note. Keep a supply of sympathy cards on hand or write a personal note on stationery.

In addition to sending a sympathy card, consider visiting in person to show support and respect for your colleague. Whether you attend the viewing, wake, funeral, or pay a shiva visit, taking the time to personally acknowledge another's loss is simply good manners. If you are unsure about religious customs for any life-cycle event, simply find someone to ask. Do not forego the opportunity to do the right thing simply because you're uncertain about what to do at a wake. Ask and show up.

If you are close to a colleague, it is appropriate to make a donation to the charity of the family's choice to honor the memory of the deceased. Typically, information about charitable donations is noted in the obituary or is available at the funeral home.

Office Etiquette:
Working with Those More Junior

The milieu of the senior attorney working with the more junior lawyer is not merely the flip side of that of the supervised working with the supervisor. While both are working to serve their common external client, the more junior is not the "client" of the more senior in the same way that the senior is the client of the junior. A different relationship of obligation exists between the senior and the junior that is in many ways more important than even a client-counselor relationship.

More senior attorneys have in their care the career development of their junior colleagues, as lawyers and as future leaders; as a result, the rules of etiquette that frame their interactions have special consequence. Senior attorneys should conduct their interactions with junior team members so as to obtain not only the best work in the short term, but also the most growth in the long run. This is true even when it appears unlikely that a junior colleague will stay associated with the work environment for many years, as some of the best potential clients are former colleagues.

How does the relationship between supervisor and supervised attorney play itself out in some specific situations? Let's go to the tape.

• "Praise publicly, criticize privately"

Into each life, a little rain must fall, and into each work relationship, a little constructive (hopefully) criticism is all but inevitable. When you as the senior attorney have such feedback to provide to the junior lawyer, how you do so is at least as important as what you say.

Attorneys are notoriously focused on the task at hand, and in so focusing can lose track of where they are and what's going on around them, sometimes quite literally. This can lead to criticism being provided loudly with the door open, in a crowded hallway, on the elevator, in the building lobby, or even at a meeting in front of clients, counterparties, and opposing counsel. Such public displays of criticism are thoughtless at best and destructive at worst; they violate the cardinal rule of etiquette in this circumstance, which is, "praise publicly, criticize privately."

Public comments about performance should consist exclusively of genuine expressions of praise; a "great job!" delivered in front of other lawyers and staff members, can buoy not only the spirits of the person to whom the accolade is directed, but also the morale of the entire office. People want to work in a place where their contributions are noticed and valued; as a leader—whether of a project, an office, or an entire firm—you have it in your treasury to dispense public praise as your coin of the realm, and should do so whenever the performance merits it.

By contrast, criticism should only be delivered privately, behind a closed door, and in a voice that won't be overheard. Nothing chills the office more than being able to tell that "so-and-so's being taken to the woodshed," because you can hear the screaming coming from the corner office. Moreover, wherever possible, criticism should be delivered in person, and not by email or voice mail.

Nobody likes conflict, and the temptation to avoid it by launching an electronic missile at a subordinate is sometimes almost irresistible, but resist you should. Errant subordinates deserve your engagement and interaction if they are to learn from their missteps, and, frankly, are entitled to the respect of a face-to-face meeting. In fact, if the temptation to avoid an in-person meeting is all but overwhelming, that's almost certainly an indication that meeting in person is precisely what the etiquette of the critique truly requires.

• Be the driver, not the whip

Related to the notion of public praise and private criticism is a stylistic point on leadership, which has an attached component of etiquette. We must each find our own management voice, and many a text on leadership can present as many convincing arguments against the "buddy" style of leadership as against the cruel taskmaster model. No matter what voice turns out to be your own, though, the etiquette of leadership suggests that you should focus on the goal, and on guiding your team toward its attainment; *ad hominem* attacks and personal invective are unlikely to get you to your destination. In all of your interactions, seek to treat everyone—most especially subordinates—with the respect and human decency that they deserve. Even the harshest bosses will be perceived as fair, if they focus their efforts properly.

• Watch the clock . . . and don't be late!

All senior team members become subject to competing demands on their time. Meetings bump against meetings; conference calls against client calls; professional obligations against personal ones. Scheduling—especially in an increasingly 24/7, Internet-paced world—becomes a nightmare (one that a healthy relationship with a competent secretary can do wonders to ease), and keeping on time and on task seems all but impossible.

Nonetheless, senior lawyers have a special responsibility to make every effort to be on time for their obligations; promptness is a point of etiquette, and a matter of respect for the time of others. All lawyers live in fear of being late for a court appearance or a filing deadline, and most dread being late for a client obligation; yet many are perfectly willing to be late for—or completely miss—office partner meetings, meetings with nonlegal staff, and the like.

Sometimes unanticipated client demands do interfere in ways that simply cannot be avoided, and, of course, the clients are paying to keep the lights on. Barring such true emergencies, though, the senior lawyer should make every possible effort to arrive for meetings on time, stay until they end, and forswear interruptions such as BlackBerries and cell phone calls.

When other demands of a less-than-urgent nature are allowed to take precedence, the clear message to everyone else in the meeting is, "My time is more important than yours." This is hardly a way to get the best out of everyone, or to make the most productive use of collaboration opportunities. Instead, an in-progress meeting may stop to admit a latecomer, who then must be caught-up on what transpired before, or may stop when a key participant walks out, bringing all progress to a halt before responsibilities can be allocated and deliverables set. Make it your goal to show up on time, stay throughout, and leave in an orderly fashion, so that all of the participants can benefit from your wisdom and insight.

• "Give us the tools, and we will finish the job"

Survey after survey shows that junior lawyers crave two things: responsibility and feedback. We've spoken above about the etiquette of criticism, but what can etiquette tell us about responsibility? Simply this: To the extent appropriate, try to approach supervisory situations in a way that makes each member of the team feel that they have something to accomplish and for which they are accountable. Provide clear direction, set concrete objectives, and require continuous reporting of progress, but, where possible, allow the workers to perform the work themselves.

• "Success has a thousand fathers, but failure is an orphan"

In the context of etiquette, perhaps this should be rephrased as, "Success has a thousand children." Many have been credited with the phrase, "There is no limit to what we can accomplish, so long as we don't care who gets the credit." The etiquette of supervision suggests that credit should be shared broadly, and not sparingly. Everyone likes to bask in the reflected glow of success; graciousness compels us to cause the glow to shine as brightly as we can, and to illuminate the lives of as many members of the team as possible.

Then again, sometimes things don't turn out quite as well as we had hoped. When that happens, a sober examination of what went wrong and to whom the failure can be traced is critical to avoiding similar mistakes in the future. That inquiry, though, and most especially its outcome, should take place quietly and without public expressions of blame or reproach whenever possible.

It may not always be practical for the senior attorney to avoid identifying the source of an error, but the etiquette of leadership amidst failure strongly suggests that the right thing to do is to acknowledge the failure and the leadership, and to foster the notion that "the buck stops here." Taking responsibility—and even blame—for the errors of those you supervise can be hard and painful. When done correctly, though, and within the context of a healthy team, it can also build loyalty and a sense of obligation not to let the same thing happen again.

• "Thank you"

Just as credit should be shared as broadly as is warranted, so should be gratitude. Because every child learns that "please" and "thank you" are the two critical phrases of rudimentary etiquette; it's shocking how many adults forget those phrases—most especially "thank you"—in their everyday lives.

Expressions of thanks go even further when made to more junior team members; they acknowledge service and sacrifice, and thus make service and sacrifice more meaningful and rewarding.

Nearly everyone has had a project come in late in the day, or a piece of work expand to require a late-night effort or a weekend trip into the office. One of the burdens that often fall upon more junior lawyers is to stay late or to work the weekend at the behest of the more senior practitioner, so that something can be "on my desk first thing in the morning" or "ready to roll on Monday," yet too few of the senior lawyers who benefit from such hard work remember to say, "Thanks for staying late," or, "I really appreciate your getting this done over the weekend." Proper etiquette requires of the supervisor an expression of gratitude for the effort of the subordinate. Just say, "Thanks."

Office Etiquette:
Working with Staff

The question of the etiquette of working with staff may be the thorniest one presented in this book, bound up as it is with issues of class (the great unmentionable in American society), seniority, even gender. Moreover, it's an issue that cuts across generations, as the most senior attorneys may well have been brought up in an age and a culture where relationships with staff were dramatically different than they are today, while the newest attorneys may never have worked in an environment where they have been asked to supervise anyone else, and may be utterly clueless as to how best to do so. Play all of this against the backdrop of legal liability for harassment and other workplace misbehaviors, and you are looking at a veritable minefield for the unprepared.

In the not-so-distant past, etiquette and custom both compelled a certain type of order on lawyer-staff relations. The lawyer was able to take on a decidedly superior role, whether of lord and master or of benevolent dictator, while staff were able to feel some reflected benefit of being associated with respected professionals and performing valued, integral roles within the lawyer's world.

After all, most lawyers didn't type their own briefs or their own contracts, weren't easily accessible outside business hours or without the intermediation of a secretary, and generally did not function alone in the professional world; a trusted staff member was basically always at hand.

Today, of course, the world has been turned upside down. No matter how hard the eldest generation of lawyers claims to have worked in their youth, study after study finds that work has expanded to fill the time allotted for its completion, and that the time so allotted has expanded to encompass all twenty-four hours of the day, and all seven days of the week. Since staff working hours have by and large not changed (except for the advent of the 'round-the-clock resource support center), this means that a large portion of a lawyer's work life will be spent working alone, or at the least without a secretary handy.

Moreover, law school graduates today arrive with years of computer experience behind them; many feel, if anything, more comfortable processing their own work than relying on anyone else to do it. Finally, they are arriving at the doorstep of a system where the traditional roles of all of the parties are completely up for grabs; more senior attorneys can no longer guide them by saying, "When I was just a young whippersnapper . . .," and more tenured staff members are often fearful that their relevance is on the wane. Into that volatile mix come junior lawyers who may feel that they need to assert themselves and their authority in order to be respected.

What can etiquette teach us, to guide us through such turbulent waters? Beyond the many employment-law-mandated requirements we could cite, here are four helpful rules to bear in mind:

• "The name of the game is . . ."

If one key to successful networking is remembering names (see "Name amnesia" in Chapter Nine), then one equally valuable tip for successful interaction with staff is to learn and remember with whom you're working. These aren't merely helpers; these are your colleagues and teammates. Imagine the manager of a baseball team not knowing his players' names, and filling in the lineup card using numbers alone; that's not the sort of manager who will lead his team to the World Series by motivating everyone to come together as one unit.

Establishing a personal connection by simply knowing and remembering staff members' names will go further than you can imagine to build the sort of respectful environment that breeds success and service; staff members will feel engaged, and not merely commanded, and you'll feel responsible for them as people, and not simply a consumer of their efforts. Knowing with whom you're working is the touchstone of polite and respectful behavior in the workplace.

• Get over yourself

Respect is earned, not compelled; to earn it, approach staff with some semblance of humility. Whether you've been practicing law for forty years or for forty-five minutes, the practice of law is what you do, not who you are, and those around you—from the managing partner to the messenger and back again—have something to teach you.

Humility does not imply supplication, nor does it compel you to be everyone's buddy; nonetheless, open your mind to the notion that those around you have their own areas of experience and expertise, and accord them the deference in those areas that is their due.

Unless you've been working as a secretary in your spare time, the secretaries in your office know more about word processing than you do now, or ever will; find a way to pass your work through them, in order to polish it to its highest luster. They also know more about how to manage a database of contacts and a calendar of obligations than you ever will; consolidate both activities in their hands.

The people who run the copy center know more about making copies and binding sets of documents than you will ever care to know; the information technology people know more about your IT systems than you can imagine; the facilities staff knows more about how to set up a conference than you ever dreamed possible. Draw on their expertise by treating everyone with respect.

• Nothing is beneath you

We've highlighted the importance of relying upon the expertise of staff, but we'd recommend not doing so to the point of personal paralysis. Because the work has now slipped the bounds of the working day, the time will come when you need to make a photocopy or to send a fax late at night or on the weekend, when there's nobody around to help you. Ask appropriate staff members to teach you the basics of what you need to know in order to function independently under such circumstances; doing so will not only engender their respect for you as a fully functioning member of the team, but will also inspire within you a greater appreciation for what your colleagues do for you.

We've seen time after time the example of a lawyer who is respected by the staff as a pitch-in player motivating staff members to want to pitch-in, as well. Making common effort in service of the common cause is a positive rule of etiquette and of leadership. When you're in the conference room with ten minutes to go before the overnight delivery service shows up to pick up your fifteen-party document distribution, collating and stuffing envelopes alongside the support staff, you'll know how much it matters to them and to the goal of client service that you were leading by example.

• Recognize contributions

Finally, recognize staff in particular for their contributions to the team effort. When a case is won, or a deal closes, too often the kudos are conferred only on the lawyers, and the vital support staff are overlooked. Doing so reinforces the notion among support staff that the lawyer-staff divide is the line between two castes; staff can easily question why they are working so hard, and so loyally, for such ungrateful employers.

By contrast, we know of lawyers who routinely single out staff members for public praise and appreciation, and who receive in return a level of hard work and loyalty that transcends anything that mere money can buy. The rule of etiquette known as "politeness" applies here; spread praise broadly, and by all means include the staff within the ambit of your public expressions of gratitude.

Clients and Client Development

As law is at its heart a service business, you might think that there is really only one rule—of etiquette, or of anything else—in dealing with existing clients, and acquiring new ones: Serve, serve, serve. Indeed, that's a terrific place to start thinking about how to interact with actual and potential clients, but it's only a starting point.

Whenever clients are asked why they like a particular lawyer or law firm, or why they have switched counsel, the answers consistently touch on matters of service, but as seen through the lens of behavior.

Clients assume technical competence; what they want is to have their calls and emails answered promptly, their deadlines met (or, if not to be met, then warned of the impending failure, with plans made for how and when their expectations will be satisfied), and to be dealt with as though their needs—and not their lawyer's—are paramount. In other words, they want to be treated with respect. Let's discuss some simple rules in the etiquette of dealing with clients—and then tackle some business devel-

43

opment situations involving potential clients, as well—to see how respectful can be translated into client satisfaction.

• Answer the phone, please

An unbelievable number of client interactions start with a phone call, one that basically says, "I need help. Can you please help me?" If at all possible, lawyers should answer their own phone. Clients are often incredibly impressed that a lawyer answers his or her own line. It conveys eagerness to help, and also a willingness to take whatever calls come, and not to dodge them.

Sometimes, of course, it's not possible to answer your own phone, because you're in a meeting, or working on an important drafting assignment or preparation session that requires quiet contemplation. During such times, it's perfectly acceptable to have your assistant answer your phone, and to be unavailable. Rather than simply leaving your assistants to fend for themselves in the face of an insistent client, however, get into the habit of agreeing upon a time at which they'll say you're expected to be free to return calls, and then try your best to stick to that time. Clients really appreciate having lawyers who are respectful enough of their clients' time to keep the appointments they make, even when the appointment in question is simply a time at which to return a call.

• Sound excited

Is this really a rule of etiquette? Perhaps not; maybe it's more of a suggestion as to deportment. Whatever it is, though, we can tell you from personal experience that excitement and eagerness—if genuine—come through on the telephone, and so do their opposites, including dread and disdain. Clients really pick up on an excited lawyer (anyone reading this from outside the profession, let us assure you that there are lots of excited, happy lawyers; they're the ones who are comfortable in their own skins), and sensing your excitement makes them want to call you. And creating clients who want to call you is called "client development." This little rule is worth writing down on a sticky note and affixing to the phone; it's that important.

• Return calls promptly

Now we're clearly back in the realm of etiquette. As a service matter, sooner is better for returning calls; surely within a business day, if at all possible within a very few hours—there's no such thing as "too soon" to return a call from anyone, but most especially a client. Remember that a call from a client is a call for your help, and the entire profession is all about help; even when you're feeling overwhelmed, you should be grateful for the call, and eager (see above) to return it.

• Respond in kind

Here's a rule of etiquette for the avoidant personality: Don't return a call with an email, unless expressly requested by the caller to do so. A call conveys so much more than an email, providing tone, pace, the ability to interact in real time, and a chance for you to affect the mental and emotional state of the caller.

Email is severely limited in its ability to do more than convey information; tone is often lost at best, or miscon-strued at worst (and yes, all of you wonderful writers who have excelled at every level of education by virtue of your superior wordsmithing abilities, this applies to you, as well; F. Scott Fitzgerald would suffer from the same infirmity, if he were writing today and electronically). There will no doubt be times when you return to your desk to find a voice mail from a client that says, "Send me an email with your availabil-ity for a meeting later this week," or something similar, but unless you're specifically asked to respond in writing, return a call with a call.

• "Return to sender . . ."

When, nonetheless, you are communicating by email, several rules of email etiquette can make your client communica-tions more effective, and thus more welcome and productive.

First and foremost, respond to emails promptly; the medium fairly compels this (indeed, sometimes we respond almost too promptly, with an unguarded reply that we wish we could recall), but lest you be confused on this point, those clients who choose to reach you in writing with the speed of email expect a prompt response; their choice of medium sig-nals their desire for service. As with returning phone calls, certainly no longer than a single day should elapse between receipt and reply; sooner (much sooner) is better.

Second, respond with brevity if you can. Bearing in mind that email often lacks tone (other than a harsh one), a brief message is more suited to the best use of the medium, conveying factual information (dates, times, names, and jersey numbers). In addition, with email now having gone mobile though the ubiquitous BlackBerry and similar handheld devices, long messages are often too difficult for clients to read. The handheld screens are small, the circumstances under which the messages are read (furtively in a meeting, or on the train to work, or at a sinfully indulgent—and completely necessary—mid-afternoon baseball game) are not conducive to careful thumbwheel manipulation and word-for-word reading, and thus the chance of misinterpretation increases exponentially.

Finally, email is forever; no matter how sure you are that it's been deleted by both sender and recipient, it's out there somewhere, on a server, in an archive, just waiting to be produced in response to a discovery request or congressional subpoena. Unless you have drafted your electronic communications with the care and forethought that you'd put into a memorandum of law or a legal opinion, the less said, the better.

• "Is this mike on?"

With so much business being transacted by phone today, the conference call has become a staple of the lawyer's life, and often that call takes place by speakerphone. Speakerphones allow you to work hands-free, keeping drafts of several transaction documents before you while you negotiate, taking notes while listening to a conversation, and perhaps including other lawyers and clients in the room with you on one side of the call while facing off against counterparties and opposing counsel on the other side. This terrific tool has its own rules of etiquette, however.

First, be sure to announce multiple parties on your end. A "roll call" at the beginning of a conference call is a very nice way to figure out who is present on the other end of the phone; you should reciprocate by announcing all of the parties on your own end, if possible. There will no doubt be circumstances when someone is a silent participant, and thus unannounced (the junior associate who is joining you for training purposes, but not being billed out to the client for the call, for example), but in general, letting everyone know who's on the line is common courtesy, as well as professionally sound behavior.

Second, pick up the handset and go off speaker when you sense the need to do so. If you are on the speakerphone with multiple people in the room with you, and a client begins to make a personal aside to you, pick up and take that portion of the conversation out of a too-public forum.

Finally, beware the "mute" button. By now, we've all likely been in circumstances where someone has believed that they have "muted" their end of the call, only to be still audible to the other participants; at best, such a technical malfunction can produce a no-harm, no-foul window into the other side of the conversation, but at worst it can reveal internal deliberations that were intended to be private, or, worse still, some snarky personal aside that was not meant to be heard. All of the adherence imaginable to the other rules of etiquette cannot undo the damage that an unintended and unmuted snide remark can do in the midst of a delicate negotiation; take appropriate care, and don't become the fodder for someone else's cautionary tale.

• Don't just be prompt, be early

We've discussed other elements of promptness elsewhere, but they all bear amplification here, when applied to meetings with clients, where they all reduce to one simple rule: Do not be late, period.

Clients deserve the utmost respect of their time, especially from those of us who happen to be charging them for our own. Strive to be super-prompt, arriving slightly early (five minutes or so should be sufficient) for every single obligation where a client is present. The discipline of planning to be early will save you when circumstances conspire to try to make you late; arriving early will also give you a moment to compose yourself, use the rest room, pop a breath mint, or just meditate. If you must be late, despite your best efforts (if, for example, you have to use any Los Angeles freeway to get to your destination, no matter what the hour of the day), then be sure you have a way to let your client know that you've been delayed, as soon as possible, so that they can use the time in ways other than contemplating how to engage other counsel.

• Client development

Finally, a few etiquette-related tips for those on the great quest for that holiest of grails, the new client. Should you be fortunate enough to have a meeting opportunity with a prospective client, four little rules of etiquette will suffice, even if you forget your own name.

First, be prepared. Know something about the people and the organization with whom you're meeting, and why you're there. This may not sound like a rule of etiquette, but of course it is; this is merely being respectful of the time of others, specifically the time that they're allotting to speak with you. If you're prepared, then you can help them to use that time productively.

Second, listen more than you speak, especially at first. Let them tell you what they want, and then be responsive to their articulated needs. This is the etiquette of deference; it's also a handy way to figure out what you want to say yourself. Formal presentations and pitches are all well and good, but nothing works quite so well as being polite enough to listen to others first.

Third, whether you say it or not, have an attitude of "please." Remember that you're the seeker, no matter how much you may feel that you're in fact being sought for your expertise and experience; many's the lawyer who has lost a potential client who simply could not abide the lawyer's arrogance. You don't need to arrive on bended knee; you must, though, remember to project an attitude of graciousness and humility, and thinking "please," even if you don't say it, will help you to do so.

Finally, say, "thank you," both verbally at the end of your meeting and in writing after you return to your office. You've just been given a great gift, namely the opportunity to demonstrate your worthiness and eagerness to help, which, if correctly perceived, may present you with a tangible monetary reward. The very least you can do is to say, "Thank you," and to do so correctly, which means not only aloud but also in a written note. Everyone appreciates being appreciated; who's to say that your own gratitude, appropriately expressed, won't be the final push that brings a new client into your practice?

Opposing Counsel

The question of how to deal with opposing counsel is a thorny one. On the one hand, these are *opposing* counsel —the people on the other side of the table, across the chasm, working every bit as hard to represent their client zealously as you are (and well they should, as their ethical obligations compel them to do so). In the heat of battle, who's to say that the rule should be anything other than "all's fair in love and war," so long as we stay within the bounds of the rules of legal ethics? Indeed, we can all point to many an example of a no-holds-barred, take-no-prisoners practitioner with whom we've gone toe-to-toe, eyeball-to-eyeball, *mano-a-mano*.

On the other hand, does the ethical duty of zealous representation actually compel us to confront opposing counsel as though we were Schwarzenegger in the last reel of any of his films (well, except for *Twins*, and perhaps *Kindergarten Cop*)? Whatever happened to the courtly manners of the bar? Is there no place left in our profession for the time-honored custom of professional courtesy?

This being, after all, a book about etiquette for

lawyers, it will surprise you not at all that we do, in fact, think that there are—or at least ought to be—rules that can guide us in our interactions with opposing counsel.

• "You catch more flies with honey . . ."

Now, we're lawyers, and we do recognize that sharp elbows are sometimes required to get through a tough negotiation or a challenging litigation; so be it. But we nonetheless subscribe to the notion that, in general, you can indeed "disagree without being disagreeable."

To the extent possible, try to keep a calm voice in interchanges with opposing counsel; avoid hyperbole and histrionics; and don't shout, scream, literally pound the table with your fist or shoe, or writhe on the floor.

At some point, such behaviors cross the line from merely aggressive to actually theatrical, and thereby lose their effect. While you're screaming bloody murder on a conference call, trust us, the other side has pushed the "mute" button and is probably laughing at how out-of-control you are. We won't go so far as to say that such tactics never work, but we will say that they work far less frequently and effectively than you might think.

• "What goes around, comes around"

In law, as in poker, there are times when you hold all the right cards (or, as they say in Texas Hold 'Em, "you have the positive nuts"); with leverage comes success, or at least the likelihood of success. But, in law as in poker, after each hand the cards are shuffled and dealt again, and leverage has a funny way of slipping away from you and crossing the table now and again.

So, conduct yourself with opposing counsel in such a manner that, if a tectonic shift happens to occur, you haven't built such a reservoir of resentment and lust for revenge that they'll be motivated to crush, kill, and destroy you and your client's position.

David tells his junior colleagues of a representation he once saw, in which a client was investing in a highly touted Internet start-up that was represented by counsel who, shall we say, possessed arrogance in direct proportion to the soaring valuations of his client. He screamed and cried and carried on in the negotiation over the initial investment, and, since he had the leverage (everyone wanted to buy into this company), he got a terrific deal for his client.

But things have a way of turning around. A couple of years later the Internet start-up needed more capital from its existing investors, and by then the worm had turned, the market had gone south, and the leverage shoe was on the other foot, and the investor who was being asked to pony up new money remembered well the abusive behavior of company counsel. Funnier still, the fellow tried it again, yelling and carrying on during conference calls, trying to scare his client and everyone else half to death. The investor sat stoically through it all, denying point after point that company counsel raised (even the reasonable ones). Don't let this happen to you.

• Communications with parties known to be represented

We all learned in our Legal Ethics course that, if you're communicating with another party whom you know to be represented by counsel, then that opposing counsel must be present for the communication, unless the opposing counsel —not the opposing party—waives the right to participate. Yet, in instance after instance, this rule is forgotten, especially in non-litigation contexts; lawyers call the other side's client directly to ask a due diligence question, or email them directly without copying their lawyers to seek a document or send a new draft, and don't seem to recognize the issue they've created.

The ethical rule against communicating directly with an opposing party known to be represented no doubt stems from an appreciation of the special ability that lawyers have, due to their superior knowledge of the law and of how it can be turned to the advantage of one side or the other, to manipulate or trap the other side when their lawyer isn't present to defend them. (One with a more cynical cast of mind might also view this rule as a sort of "lawyers' full employment act," but that strikes us as less than charitable.)

So, it's easy for us to reiterate the ethical rule as a rule of etiquette, as well: Don't communicate with the other side of a case or deal, who you know to be represented, without going through their lawyer.

This means that, when your client calls you and says, "Call so-and-so on the other side, and ask such-and-such," the only right answer is to reply, "Great, I'll call their lawyer and ask if we can put together an all-hands conference call." Similarly, when it's time to send a draft contract out to all parties, the other side's lawyers must be copied if their client is a recipient; if you don't have their contact information, you may call or email the opposing party directly to ask for contact details, but nothing else. Follow the ethical rule, and you'll be a model of good etiquette.

What happens, though, when you slip up, and despite your best efforts inadvertently send something without copying opposing counsel? Admit your mistake immediately; call the lawyer on the other side and apologize; and then send a personal, handwritten note to reiterate your regret. This doesn't have to be an over-the-top, rend-your-own-garment note; a simple, "I apologize once more for my omission" will serve very nicely. Doing so is not a sign of weakness; the weakness of your error speaks for itself, and to err is human, after all. Rather, it's a sign of self-confidence, and a way of re-leveling the playing field; you're taking the other side down from the moral high ground on which you've placed them through your own actions, and thus benefiting your client.

Outside Advisors

Lawyers are frequently called upon to work with third parties in order to accomplish an assignment for a client.

Over the course of a day, you may wind up helping a forensic accountant gather materials to analyze a complicated commercial litigation; chatting with tax advisors on a conference call to help structure a complicated international acquisition; speaking with a caregiver who is helping an aged client with a healthcare challenge; collaborating with an environmental consultant while dealing with a real property matter; or just arranging to have the local copy shop duplicate six banker's boxes of deposition exhibits. These are ordinary-course commercial transactions and business relationships among service providers; yet, even here, there are rules of conduct and of business etiquette that can help you to achieve better results for yourself and your clients. What are they?

• We're all in the same boat

At first blush, it may seem to you that outside advisors are just vendors, and are there to do no more than serve you at your pleasure. The temptation to transfer the stress and strain of your own work onto their backs may be enormous; after all, you're getting last-minute calls from clients posing impossible challenges and making unreasonable demands, so why shouldn't you do the same when the shoe is on the other foot? Sad but true, everyone is tempted to kick the dog from time to time.

Here's why you should not give in to the temptation to be anything less than gracious in your dealings with outside advisors: Both you and the outside advisor are striving to reach the same goal, serving your mutual client. The etiquette of the situation, therefore, suggests that you treat the advisor as a part of your own team, and not as someone across the table. Doing so gives you a key to unlock the door to better client service for the client you both share.

An outside advisor who is treated with courtesy and respect—even before that respect has been earned through independent action—is more likely to rise to the occasion and perform up to the level that you require, and that, in turn, will make your life far easier than any flogging before the mast, no matter how cathartic. Outside advisors are no different than your own internal team members; they respond to the same signs of respect, awards of credit, and expressions of gratitude. In the words of the movie of the same title, "pay it forward," and extend to your outside advisors and vendors the same courtesy that you'd want to receive yourself.

• Listen and learn

Beyond mere responsiveness and performance, outside advisors and vendors have a perspective of their own to add, and can educate you in how to meet client expectations more fully; thus, the second rule of etiquette is to open your ears, and listen politely to what third-party vendors have to say. After all, they see a variety of different lawyers and other service providers in their own work; they know what succeeds, and what fails. You can learn much from those who are interacting with your clients on a different level; polite inquiry with an attitude of deference and respect will yield a pearl or two of wisdom someday that will improve your own client service and repay your kindness many times over.

• Start spreading the news

Finally, outside advisors can be their own pathways to business development, and thus are worthy of being treated as worth their weight in gold. You never know when that environmental consultant will be speaking with some prospective client of whom you've never even dreamt, and hearing about that prospect's woes with other counsel. When that happens, you want to be in a position for that advisor to recount what a terrific relationship they've seen you have with your clients and those clients' whole teams, including service providers.

Despite the advances of technology and the retreats of advertising, law is still very much a business based on personal contacts; to rise to the level of being a client's trusted advisor, you often need to start by being recommended by another. Word-of-mouth is the most important client development tool you have. Make sure that the positive buzz about you is heard from all directions, including outside service providers, by treating them all in so respectful a manner that speaking well of you becomes second nature to them.

After Hours:
Office Events

Socializing as part of your work life enables you to enjoy time with colleagues, staff members, and clients in a more relaxed environment. After-hours events blend work and leisure; on the one hand, you are spending time with work colleagues; on the other hand, you are outside the office, at a sports event, birthday party, or other celebration. As a result, it can be a little confusing in terms of what's appropriate and what's inappropriate.

The golden rules of etiquette (see Chapter Twelve) apply at all times. Good manners do not take a holiday simply because you are socializing outside the office, whether with colleagues, clients, or potential clients.

Respond In a Timely Manner

When you receive an invitation, check the date on your calendar and determine if you can attend. One of the easiest ways to show courtesy to others is to respond in a timely manner to invitations. An invitation that requests an R.S.V.P. means, please respond "yes" or "no" by a date certain. An invitation that says "regrets only" means just that: Only respond if you cannot attend; otherwise we will assume that you will be present.

Making office staff chase you down for an answer is poor behavior. No matter how busy you may be, respond and keep your commitment. If your work or travel schedule prohibits a prompt response, delegate the responsibility to your professional assistant.

Determine Who Is Invited to the Event

If an invitation is addressed to you only, then you are the only invitee. If you and your spouse or partner or "and guest" are listed on the address line, then you are both invited. If your name and the words "and family" appear on the address line, then, by all means, bring the children along. In any event (no pun intended), do not bring an uninvited guest to an event. If you have any questions, simply ask the individual organizing the event for guidance.

Understand Who Will Be at the Event

It helps to prepare for an office event if you know who may be there. Is this event for lawyers only? Lawyers and staff? Everyone's families? Will firm clients be present? If so, will any of your clients be present? These are worthwhile questions to ask in order to be prepared to socialize and make everyone comfortable.

Fashionably Late versus Inexcusably Late

For large parties or other group gatherings with a cocktail hour preceding the event, fashionably late means that you can arrive up to fifteen minutes after the stated start time. After fifteen minutes you enter the domain of inexcusably late.

For sit-down dinners, ascertain from the host or hostess about the start time in order to determine what fashionably late means. For some individuals, a stated time to begin dinner is the time the event begins. Period. You don't want to walk into a room with everyone seated and enjoying their appetizers. Ask beforehand to avoid embarrassment.

For theater performances, lectures, and the like, arrive ten minutes early and leave ample time to find your seat, chat a few moments, and then enjoy the show. You do not want to be one of the latecomers seated at the discretion of the manager, particularly when you are attending an event as part of your firm.

Appropriate Attire

Should you have any question about the appropriate attire for an event, call beforehand and ask. In most cases, office events take place directly after work and this presupposes that business attire or business casual, depending on your office, is both expected and acceptable. However, if you are struggling with the precise definition of "casual chic" or "festive attire," then ask before the event to avoid embarrassment to yourself and your host.

Never wear anything too revealing or risqué. Anything too tight, too revealing, or too short may be great for personal time, but you do not want to be remembered by your colleagues or clients for being the person who wore the unusual outfit. Your goal is to be remembered for your great attitude, not your bizarre attire.

Tips for Socializing with Ease

While entire books have been written about how to navigate social events, the following are some useful tips to keep in mind. Susan RoAne's *Secrets of Savvy Networking* provides funny, in-depth advice for those in need of detailed information.

• Be the host (even if you're not the host)

One of the best ways to take control of a social situation is to pretend that you are hosting the event and in charge of making people feel comfortable. This is a great trick and it really works. Rather than stand by idly, make yourself the official greeter and seater. Make it a point to say hello, introduce yourself, and—if the event is open seating—invite someone to sit with you. When you stop focusing on yourself and start focusing on others, you will be amazed at the quality of interactions that follow.

• Make introductions

People assume that everyone knows everyone else. This is a huge assumption to make, particularly at very large law firms. Act as the informal emcee and make sure you introduce people. Never assume that Person A knows Person B. Here's how to do it: "John, I want you to meet Fred, the new tax associate who just started with us. John is a senior associate in the litigation department. Fred, meet John."

• Name amnesia

You can't remember a person's name. You're embarrassed. They look so familiar, but you don't know where you know them from. You're too young to have Alzheimer's and your head injury healed years ago. What do you do? Don't panic. Everyone forgets names. We've been known to forget our own child's name from time-to-time (tip: "hey, you" works fine). Simply turn to the person in question, smile, and say, "I am so sorry, but please tell me your name again." Then— here's the key—stop, look at the person and really listen to the name they tell you. Then repeat the person's name and say, "Fran, that's right. Nice to see you again." If you're really good, you'll repeat the name in your head a few times and try to create a connection, like Fran with the deep tropical tan, or something like that.

• Pay attention

When you are engaged in a conversation with one or more people, make those people the focus of your attention. No looking at your watch. No roving eye to see if someone better walks into your line of vision. People notice when someone's attention is drifting; it's impolite. Make it a point to pay full attention to the person in front of you before scanning the room for friends.

• Breaking into conversations

It can be very daunting to walk into a room of strangers and expect to engage people in conversation. This can be particularly hard when people are gathered in small groups and seem to be having a jolly time without you. Tip: Avoid breaking into pairs engaged in conversation. Typically, two people standing close with their heads together are having a personal conversation. Unless one of them catches your eye and beckons you to join them, look for groups of three or more. Stand at the periphery and try to make eye contact. This is where the edict to "be the host" can be so important. Look for someone to make eye contact, smile, and ask you to join them.

• Jokes

Jokes are no laughing matter when they hit upon the forbidden topics of politics, race, religion, or sexual preference. If you have a good sense of humor and can remember a few "clean" jokes, then joke to your heart's content. Casual observations of a humorous nature are always appropriate. However, be cautious when telling off-color jokes. What if you are the recipient of an off-color joke? It's the height of bad manners to put another person in the uncomfortable position of having to react to something tasteless or offensive. This can be further complicated when the joke-teller is someone in a position of power over you. Do you risk offending the managing partner by saying, "I find that offensive"? Use good judgment in these cases. When a peer tells an off-color joke, express your displeasure politely. "That's not appropriate and it's not funny, Jane." If the joke-teller is a senior person, acknowledge quietly and move on.

• Furnishing business cards

A lawyer should always carry business cards because networking opportunities can happen anywhere. There is, however, an art to furnishing a business card and some do's and don'ts. For example, furnish a business card after you have spoken with a person for at least a few minutes and established a connection. Simply throwing business cards on tables or leaving them for the wait staff to find is not effective. Instead, finish your discussion and say, "I'd love to follow up with you; do you have a business card?" That's the opportunity to hand your business card to the person. Take a moment and look at the card; don't simply put it away without another look. Examine the card briefly and, if possible, make a sincere comment ("that's a nice design," or, "what a cool job title," or something that shows you are paying attention). Business cards should not be furnished at funerals, during hospital visits, and anywhere that feels inappropriate. Not only can furnishing business cards in hospitals or funeral parlors be construed as soliciting clients (and a violation of the Rules of Professional Conduct), but it's just poor manners.

• Exiting with grace

How can you extricate yourself from a conversation? Here are some tried-and-true exit lines: "I'm going to refresh my drink," "I have to see if this call is the transplant surgeon (hold phone in hand)," or "Excuse me, it's been a pleasure chatting."

Specific Socializing Scenarios
The Office Holiday Party

It may be "the most wonderful time of the year," but it's also the time of the year when the most egregious behavior happens. This is, in part, due to holiday cheer and an abundance of eggnog. When you attend the office holiday party, keep in mind a few common-sense rules of etiquette:

- Enjoy a drink or two, but don't become drunk. Once you are inebriated, your ability to make good decisions about proper behavior is greatly reduced. You may not remember what you did when you were drunk, but your colleagues and staff members will remember forever.

- Consider serving as a designated driver or—if you know you will be consuming alcohol—have a designated driver on hand or arrange transportation home. Not only is it impolite to drive while intoxicated, it's also illegal.

- Dress appropriately (see above).

- Engage in polite conversation and learn the art of small talk. *What Do I Say Next? Talking Your Way to Business and Social Success* by Susan RoAne contains excellent advice to help you converse with ease. Conversation topics to avoid: politics, religion, money, or sexuality.

The Summer Associate Event

Many mid-sized and large law firms offer summer associate events and ask attorneys to participate and represent the firm. Whether it is a cocktail party, dinner event, or family picnic, you may be asked to attend, represent the firm, and meet summer associates.

Your role, as an attorney, is to represent the firm in the best light possible. This means:

- Engage summer associates in pleasant conversation;
- Ask about their law school experiences; and
- Answer questions as candidly as possible while remembering that you are a representative of the firm.

The Client Social Event

Clients may invite you to a holiday party, a product launch, a social dinner with spouses, or a charity golf outing. Similarly, you may be in a position to invite clients to socialize outside regular office hours. These types of events offer excellent opportunities to solidify relationships in an informal environment. All of the aforementioned tips apply to client social events: Dress appropriately, drink in moderation (or not at all), engage in pleasant conversation, and be sure to thank the host or hostess afterwards.

An important aspect of client entertaining is to reciprocate in a timely manner. Hence, if you are invited to a holiday party, then be sure to calendar a date to call after New Year's and initiate a lunch together and so forth. If you are new to client entertaining, seek help from a mentor or more senior attorney. It's poor etiquette to have a one-sided social entertainment agenda.

The Farewell Party

One of your colleagues is leaving the firm and there is a party, whether a cake in the conference room or dinner at a nearby restaurant. If your schedule permits, take the time to attend—even for a brief amount of time—and wish your colleague well. It is good manners to acknowledge another's transition. Furthermore, keeping in touch with former colleagues may also be a great networking experience for you either in the event that you, too, seek to make a transition, or in the event that you want to cultivate new business.

Express Your Thanks

After any social event, it is appropriate for you to seek out the person who planned and produced the event to say, "Thank you, you did a good job." The hours of behind-the-scenes work to produce a firm-wide holiday party, summer associate event, or any celebration are enormous and nerve-wracking. You need not write a formal thank-you note, but a sincere verbal "thank you" and an email the next day can go a long way in making a person feel valued.

One final note: If any detail of the event was not to your satisfaction (the food choices were inadequate, the room was too loud, the sound system deficient), save the criticism for later. Public criticism, as well as written criticism, is never polite and always hurtful. If you have something constructive to say, make time to take the person aside afterwards and express yourself civilly in person with the office door closed.

After Hours:
Out on Your Own

Good manners extend beyond one's office hours. Out on your own, you are still bound by the golden rules of etiquette. As an officer of the court and a representative of the legal profession in your community, you have a responsibility to project a level of professionalism and civility at all times.

Your behavior will reflect upon you, your employer, as well as the profession generally. Therefore, always exercise sound judgment when it comes to questions of behavior. By and large, this means:

• Exercise discretion at all times

No one is asking a lawyer to lead a life of monk-like abstinence in duty to the profession. You will entertain clients, family, and friends (not necessarily all together), attend bachelor or bachelorette parties, and otherwise engage in an active, engaging social life. Moderation is the key. Indulge and blow off steam in a socially appropriate way. Damning photos, blog entries, or newspaper articles should not trumpet your exploits. Nor should your reputation among your peers evince the belief that you are inappropriate or otherwise unseemly in your private life.

• Drink in moderation

While enjoying alcohol is typically part and parcel of after-hours socializing, keep in mind that you ought to drink in moderation and never lose control. Not only is drunkenness an unattractive state of being, it leads to patently illegal activities, including driving while under the influence. Consume alcohol in moderation and maintain your reputation among peers and outsiders alike.

• Keep your word

When you promise to attend an event, contribute to a charity, or offer help, be reliable and worthy of one's trust. Avoid saying "yes" and then backing out of obligations. Instead, be honest and forthright about your time and resources before making a commitment. People will respect a person who takes on fewer obligations but follows through thoroughly more than the individual who says "yes" and does not fulfill his or her commitments. Your trustworthiness is important and your reputation in these matters will extend beyond the profession.

• Volunteer within your community

Offering your services pro bono, serving on a board of directors for a community initiative, or volunteering your time for a cause that impassions you, are all wonderful ways of giving back and showing respect for those in your community. Take the time, even early in your legal career, to find a volunteer opportunity that interests you and get involved.

The Etiquette of Changing Jobs

Throughout your career there will be many opportunities to change firms, agencies, corporations, even professions. Retention and attrition studies bear out the fact that lawyers change jobs with some degree of frequency. A study by the NALP Foundation titled, "Keeping the Keepers II: Mobility and Management of Associates," reported that within the first two years of practice, nearly a quarter of the associates at law firms of all sizes have moved on. After five years, more than half of those hired out of law school have left their original firms.

With the knowledge that the legal profession is increasingly mobile, be open to the possibility of change. Networking serves many purposes, both in terms of personal fulfillment and professional practicality. Maintaining ties with college and law school classmates, law firm alums, and friends will help you explore other career options when the time is ripe.

Because so many positions are filled through word-of-mouth, it makes sense to foster those connections on a regular basis. With that in mind, be sure to tend your network of contacts with social lunches, friendly telephone calls and emails, as well as holiday correspondence. While you should not be nice for the sake of an ulterior motive, you should keep your contacts apprised of your career path generally. As networking expert Susan RoAne says, "You never know."

In particular, treat legal search professionals (headhunters) with respect when they contact you. Take headhunters' calls and speak briefly and politely no matter how busy you may be. You may not be interested in a different job opportunity today, but your career plans may change. If you are pleased with your employment situation today simply say, "Thanks for calling, but I'm happy with my situation right now." Burning bridges by being rude, sarcastic, or nasty will not benefit you in the long run, because you cannot know what the future holds.

Job change and etiquette are not mutually exclusive concepts. It is possible—and preferable—to transition from one employer to another while maintaining good manners. The following are some suggestions for leaving an employer on good terms.

• Never denigrate a former employer

Even if you left under less-than-optimal circumstances, never denigrate a former employer. Short-circuit any negative commentary by saying, "It wasn't a good fit," or, "I was looking for a different type of practice environment."

• Never denigrate a former employee

Avoid speaking negatively about former colleagues or staff professionals. First, you never know who another person knows or is related to, and unkind words will, no doubt, travel far. Second, nothing is gained by tarnishing another person's good name. Finally, bad-mouthing a former employee could result in legal action. In short, do not speak ill of the departed.

• Give appropriate notice before your departure (but be prepared to depart the day you announce your new position)

Give your employer at least four weeks' notice; however, you should be prepared to leave your office the day of your announcement. While some firm policies will vary (and certainly circumstances of departures will vary greatly and cannot be generalized here), you should assume that you may be asked to depart the premises the day of your announcement. Therefore, prepare carefully so your exit—should it happen more suddenly than you thought—is as dignified as possible.

• Adhere to the Rules of Professional Conduct regarding client files

Whether you leave to join another firm or to start your own practice, adhere to the Rules of Professional Conduct pertaining to client files and client confidentiality. You may not copy client files or other information. You may not contact clients for the purpose of soliciting them to change firms before actually leaving your current employer.

Failure to adhere to the rules in your jurisdiction is not only a breach of the Rules of Professional Conduct, but a poor reflection on you as an individual. Before switching employers, review the Rules and be sure to adhere to them carefully so as to avoid any conflicts.

The Golden Rules of Etiquette

We've considered etiquette for the legal practitioner in a wide range of settings, and seen many examples of how proper etiquette can make a lawyer's life smoother and more pleasant, as well as examples of how the absence of etiquette can lead to disagreeable, even disadvantageous, outcomes.

We hope that, at this point in our tale, the reasons to integrate politeness and good manners into your everyday work life are clear and compelling, and that the manner in which to do so has been amply demonstrated. Still, we would like to leave you with a set of guidelines to help you know what to do in almost any situation, or to know why you should act in a particular way, so that you can deduce the appropriate behavior yourself. We call these the "Golden Rules of Etiquette."

Etiquette is empathy.

The first and most important Golden Rule of Etiquette is the "golden rule" itself: Do unto others as you would have them do unto you. Whether you learned this principle from its Old Testament origins, from its New Testament revival, from another of the many religious and secular sources that incorporate this notion, or just from plain old-fashioned common sense, if you can internalize this fundamental concept, then you're already more than halfway to your destination in any situation that demands a well-mannered response or behavior.

All we're really encouraging is that each of us take the time to place ourselves in the shoes of another (the colleague with whom we're working on a case, the client who's waiting for an answer, the opposing counsel who's across the table from us in a deal, the stranger in the elevator), and then act in a way that makes the person comfortable, as we ourselves would want to be comfortable in those circumstances. Most questions of etiquette truly can be resolved by making them into simple questions of empathy, without knowing a single other "rule."

Etiquette is also respect.

Our empathic approach presumes that we would want to be treated in the shoes of another with respect—not for our position, rank, seniority, wealth, status, or caste, but rather for ourselves as a fellow human being. The notion of etiquette would be turned on its head, if we were to imagine etiquette as a set of behaviors founded on the notion that the way people want to be treated is with contempt, derision, or dismissiveness.

Etiquette as respect does not attach merely to people,

but also to everything about their situation: their time, their responsibilities, the competing demands to which they are subject, their role within an organization or a community or a family.

Etiquette is a social lubricant.

Etiquette makes it possible for people who don't have their own independent relationships of trust and respect with one another to nonetheless interact with a minimum of friction, because they each do what's more or less expected in any given circumstance. Such a lubricant can help lead to true respect, and later to actual trust, as the parties build confidence in one another over a longer course of interaction. Without etiquette (even the *ad hoc* variety based on empathy without set rules), our mercurial natures could easily undermine confidence, and leave us isolated and ineffective.

Etiquette disarms.

Etiquette makes it more difficult for counterparties to summon outrage or anger or raised voices in service of their argument. A polite and quiet approach to tense interactions can create either an induced sense of complacency or intense frustration and disorientation on the other side of the interchange; either can create opportunities to turn a situation to the benefit of the more well-behaved party.

Etiquette conveys forethought.

We all look smarter than we are when that extra instant taken to manage an interaction with a modicum of grace suggests that we know what we're doing, what effect we're having on others, and that we're mature and careful enough to handle anything that comes our way. Etiquette can help us not merely rise to the occasion, but also to create occasions that rise to us.

Etiquette is not an altruistic behavior.

In fact, it's just as much about self-interest as it is concerned with anyone else. Because etiquette comforts the recipient of well-mannered behavior, eases the path, and builds confidence, its application necessarily benefits the practitioner.

Conclusion

We very much hope that these *Modern Rules of Business Etiquette* help to guide you in the many circumstances in which you will no doubt find yourself, where well-mannered behavior may be the difference between success and failure. We trust that this resource has done nothing more than to reinforce your own best tendencies and good sense; from time to time, we all need to see the right thing to do written out for us, simply to confirm that we've not been made crazy by the insane pace and pressure of our modern world. Rather than codifying a crusty old set of rules, we would like to believe that these more organic principles can reflect the best elements of professionalism and common sense that have been part of the practice of law since the start, embodying respect for clients, colleagues, fellow practitioners, and society. We look forward to crossing paths with all of you . . . politely.

For Further Reading

- Forni, P.M. *Choosing Civility: The Twenty-Five Rules of Considerate Conduct.* New York: St. Martin's Press, 2002.
  Professor P.M. Forni of Johns Hopkins University offers a true gem for readers. Forni's twenty-five rules for connecting effectively with others is a model for well-mannered behavior in all situations.

- Fox, Sue. *Etiquette for Dummies.* New York: Wiley Publishing, 1999.
  Part of the popular For Dummies series, Sue Fox's book uses humor to cover the gamut of etiquette situations including how to communicate graciously at home and at work, and proper behavior at weddings and formal events.

- Post, Peggy and Peter Post. *The Etiquette Advantage in Business (2nd edition).* New York: HarperCollins Publishers, 2005.
  This book provides excellent general information for business etiquette in the workplace, in social settings, with clients, and throughout the interview process.

- Post, Peggy. *Everyday Etiquette: Practical Advice for Social Situations at Home and on the Job.* New York: HarperPaperbacks, 1999.
  Peggy Post offers practical advice for a range of situations, from silverware to thank-you notes, replying to invitations, making condolence calls, and other day-to-day issues.

- Post, Peggy. *Excuse Me, But I Was Next . . . How to Handle the Top 100 Manners Dilemmas.* New York: HarperCollins Publishers, 2006.

  Peggy Post catalogues the top 100 etiquette questions with simple, concise answers.

- RoAne, Susan. *What Do I Say Next?* New York: Warner Books, 1997.

  This informative, funny guide teaches you the secrets of talking your way to business and social success. RoAne addresses how to navigate social settings with ease.

- RoAne, Susan. *How to Work a Room.* New York: Warner Books, 1989.

  A wonderful, witty discussion of how to socialize and put yourself, and others, at ease.

- Shipley, David and Will Schwalbe. *Send: The Essential Guide to Email for Office and Home.* New York: Alfred A. Knopf, 2007.

  This primer on email communications offers important information on email etiquette for business.

Index

About the Authors

Donna Gerson is a contributing editor for *Student Lawyer* magazine. She is the author of several books on legal career issues, including *Choosing Small, Choosing Smart, Building Career Connections*, and the forthcoming *Asked and Answered* series. Donna graduated from the University of Pennsylvania, earned her law degree from Temple University Beasley School of Law, and also has an M.L.I.S. degree from the University of Pittsburgh. She is licensed to practice law in the Commonwealth of Pennsylvania.

David Gerson is a partner in the Pittsburgh office of Morgan, Lewis & Bockius LLP, where he practices in the firm's Business & Finance Practice Group. His practice focuses on representing financial and strategic buyers and sellers in mergers and acquisitions, as well as on equity offerings and securities compliance matters. David earned his undergraduate degree from the University of Pennsylvania and his law degree from Harvard Law School.